PERFORMANCE ANXIETY

JANE KING

PERFORMANCE ANXIETY

NEW AND SELECTED POEMS

PEEPAL TREE

First published in Great Britain in 2013
Peepal Tree Press Ltd
17 King's Avenue
Leeds LS6 1QS
UK

ISBN 13: 9781845232306

The poems selected from *Fellow Traveller* were first published by Sandberry Press, Jamaica, West Indies, 1994. The poems selected from *Into the Centre* were published in Castries in 1993.

Some of these poems have appeared in the following publications: *Anthology: Twenty Years of Literary Achievement 1979-1999, Atlanta Review, Caribbean Poetry Now, Caribbean Review of Books, Creation Fire*, *Confluence*, *CRNLE Reviews Journal, Eye to Eye – Women, The Graham House Review, The Heinemann Book of Caribbean Poetry, Kyk-over-al*, *The Literary Review, Massachusetts Review, Mississippi Review, The New Voices*, *Poetry Wales, Roseau Valley and Other Poems for Brother George Odlum, Sunsong Tide Rising* and *Wheel and Come Again*.

Supported using public funding by
ARTS COUNCIL
ENGLAND

CONTENTS

Performance Anxiety

To Kendel, Dele, Dara and Daniel

PERFORMANCE ANXIETY

SAME CIRCUS, SECOND YEAR

The golden ring, red velvet chairs,
the dust, the dark, the night:
Mikel at two is still enthralled by eerie circus light

The eldest of the dancing girls who balance on the balls
is halfway up steep sloping ramp
when suddenly she falls
she's caught by hired local men in tired velvet clothes
it's not rehearsed, it isn't fun

her face a mask of fear
bravura of her sequined thong
net bodysuit that cannot hide
the blubbering of her rear

Three once-white ducks are crammed into
a cage with muddy floor
the toddlers gravitate to them
Mikel asks what they're for

To lay the eggs to feed the snakes
and what are the snakes for?
To put their heads in a lady's mouth…

Then what's the lady for?

Oh, we're frightened, we are weary
we are hungry, sick and sore
and the crowd calls out for more
always
the crowd calls
out
for more

THE PERFORMER'S NIGHT TERROR

Bed is a very high place.
Short of breath. Wet hands
can't grip to balance.
Look at Death.
His teeth. His eyes.
Open so wide
to crunch on every fear you try to hide.
Night horror's teeth will
strip you to the bone.

Sleep is a circus ring.
Whole world stands around
grinning.
No-one should know this vulnerability
you told yourself.
But they crowd round.
It's what they want to see.
You sweat and twist and panic
and they grin.

Their eyes. Their teeth.
They're Death's.
They're closing in.

POSSESSED

Something has cursed the local tomcats:
all day as well as night they howl
those bone-juddering wails. They prowl
our house, seeking Miss Si,
who hides.

Miss Si is pregnant.
Doesn't want to play.
Hides herself in a bookshelf all day.

Her kitten perches on our bed to see
what unnatural acts we
might perform.

I dreamt this once in only slightly
nastier form.

The cat was dead.
Beside her severed head
another fucked the putrefying corpse
with great enjoyment and perhaps
unnecessary force.

GEOGRAPHY FOR ROBERT

We return
because we must
to sparkling harbour, Castries' dust,
the market bright with makambou, pumpkin, lime
seasoning peppers, various mangoes, thyme,
the reek of garbage
piled up coconut shells
little dark shops
saltfish and other smells;

to quiet La Toc, which as children we'd comb
discovering tunnels, old guard houses, secret homes
watching the lightning crash on the black sea
as thunder storms raced on to Martinique.

We will return to where we were before
the moulding hands finalised our shapes
before they fixed us in this potter's field
patterned by our landscapes.

We will return because adult despair
may lighten with a glimpse of what we saw
before we even knew how solitary we were.

In this dark time
as drought devours our land,
La Toc, Vigie, the market
help us understand.

In blinding snapshot flashes
when the harbour's suddenly cleaner
buses wood and brighter
the cruise ship's a Bequia schooner
heavy bare-breasted women squat

squelching piles of clothes to bleach
on river rocks
below the bridges by the bends
in Canaries and Anse la Raye

and we are innocent as clay…

MANCHINEEL

The sapodilla tree's for sitting in
the mangoes and siwet, however sour,
but pretty manchineel's bright leaves burn
and tiny corrosive green apples kill.
Don't ever touch the manchineel.

The languid afternoon's for rests
fresh-bathed children taken for walks
white socks, pennies to spend
tamarind balls, salt prunes, always
the salt, the sour, the sweet

and the awakening

to know
the apple that she gave to him was real
was
manchineel

THE MOTHERSIDE

No wonder they thought Fate was female.
That old trio – the mother spinning birth,
the two-faced beauty measuring the thread
while tempting us to love the things of earth,
and the gloating crone who cuts us off,
sniggering as she snips: *Bang bang! You're dead.*
The female Trinity.

The cave that we all come from,
the tunnel we go through.
The grave we have to rise from,
living we're forced to do.

Recreated in the ordinary
by the mother in your house
saying, *Eat now!* and *Go to bed!*
and *You may not go out!*
Who orders your whole life for you,
says what you may and must not do –
the one who gave you life.

No wonder we fear females
when those who gave us birth
by giving it give our death too, and
orders for time on earth.

And every earthly mother knows
her instructions incomplete,
old wives' tales generated
while thinking on your feet
with a soup pot in one hand
when a child keeps asking *Why?*
a mother, irritated yells:
Because if you do, you'll die!

The prime source of our negation
is the one who says *You may*,
who feeds us into darkness
by thrusting us to day.

THE PEARL DIVER

Sometimes a soul swoops through sleep
like a pearl diver,
sweeping through obscure deeps,
up and down through water,

sometimes still seeing Atlantis below,
its strange hills and valleys
where, today, cars like censers go
puffing sweet smoke.

A fragment of a dream,
and the soul's mission
to catch it in midstream
to interpret the vision.

Down to a cave in mountainside,
its entrance hidden,
we're pulled by an underworld tide
to horror bidden,

full of dead children, and every child
talking in its sleep,
broken bleeding babbling and wild,
no secrets to keep.

Above are chessboard floors
whose black and white
must be crawled to reach the doors
leading down and round

the old slow spiral. Even the orchard full of birds
has patches of shade
and patches of light and a voice speaking words
like a gift to be taken to daylight.

The pearl-diver's clutch is frail
as he breaks the surface,
swinging up through true light,
as light and darkness sickeningly reverse,

and the sea's blacktopped,
the dream submarine sinking
down like a hearse,
coffins of a dream.

The surface swallows light.
The vision's gone.
The emptiness of daytime's bright,
the soul alone.

His task, remembering,
the pearl-diver must bring
Atlantis' secret to day's light
and make it sing.

MEDITATION

Lord, I beg you, give to me
the rooted calmness of a tree,
the unimaginable serenity
of rock, or deep dark water.

Now, strangely, it occurs to me
that they have turmoils we can't see.
To fly or mouse, perhaps even we
seem placid as eternity.

THE PERFORMER'S LOVE POEM

Say you'll meet me darling
some place we both know well
where the leather beat of bat wings
isn't wafting me to hell
where the breezes are not bringing us
the Gotham guano smell
where I'm not afraid their squeaky claws
will tangle in my hair
oh my darling, say you'll meet me
if I find my way there…

PERFORMERS ARE HOLY

The actor who lets you see
the tears that in real life he'd die
to hide, so we can cry,
releases our sorrow painlessly.

The clown who falls down
so we can laugh
your fears to scorn
if temporarily.

Lao Tse's wise man who,
thinking quietly at home,
affects the lives of others
for a thousand miles around

The bum living on the street
who becomes part of the scenery
who redeems life with our fleet-
ing: there but for the grace of god go I.

The slack, striated belly of the stripper:
This is my body, which was given
for you and for many
for the commission of sins

The world's a temple where
on every street corner
some holy performer
is giving his life for us.

PERFORMERS ARE HOLY SIDE 2

It used to bother me when they said that God
made us to know him, love him and serve him.
It made our creation seem something of a whim
and it was difficult as a child to be overawed
by the concept of a being who needed so much laud.
A bit like the he-made-us-in-his-own-image thing
which seemed to justify so much bad seeing
because we all have somewhere a great need to be adored.

But walking down a brash Manhattan street one day
it occurred to me that the whole world really is a play.
God's into theatre, making all the scenes, casting
the roles, doing sets, lighting, costumes, in a lasting
whole. He needs us as an audience, needs comments from us.
Lord, I'm sorry that I was so slow. You are to be adored.

PERFORMER AFTER THE TROPICAL STORM

Last night the wind blew
rain drove in
the banana fields were flattened
the power lines blown down
the water pipes from the reservoir washed away

The town blurred under feet
of mud and garbage
rivers broke banks
sweeping men away

Despite the weather satellites
the global television
we had no warning,
only that a tropical depression

was approaching.
We woke to find our land
devastated by a storm
nothing prepared us for its coming

I do not know how to say
all this to you.

THE OTHER SEA ALMOND WOMEN AFTER THE STORM

These weren't the trees that Walcott saw.
These almond women on the other shore
faced west – the Caribbean calm.
They had seen rain before.
Water dripped serenely over their green,
a thirst-quenching, regular drenching.
Tears were not the worst they had seen.
Storms had passed over them,
strengthening as they moved west.

All but this last one
which reversed and came back
and the sea they'd faced so serenely
turned on them in fury,
slapped them with storm surges,
submerged them, threw at them
all the flotsam it could find
and finally receded

leaving behind leaves burned
brown and dry and yearning.
They stood hunched miserably
the sea's ageing wives stripped
of one more layer of skin,
one less protective layer
to stop the craziness getting in

ON WHETHER IT HAS TO HAVE PALM TREES TO BE CARIBBEAN POETRY

It's easier when far from home to note
the things around us – people, traffic noises.
The buildings of Manhattan burn as bright

as breadfruit tree candles incandesce
in evening light, but breadfruit tree candles,
like the late sun-lit mango lamps which dress

the trees in any ordinary yard, are kindled
quite ordinarily. Sit on the steps to watch them glow,
listening to the neighbourhood's old scandals.

THE PERFORMER GETS SOME COMFORT FROM A TREE

A tree told me that nourishment
is never very far from where we are,
that it is our most delicate filaments
that force the dust and rock aside and travel far
to tap the water, mine the minerals we need,
that it is our most vulnerable tips, like leaves
so casually blown, that search the air, like seeds
so tiny, bravely grow, whatever one believes.

The tree said: Know, you must sit still and slow.
Everything you need to grow is all around,
it's hidden in the rocks in the hard ground,
it's in the harsh and mocking wind. You know
you cannot strain and fight to dig these out.
What's softest, most vulnerable, conquers drought.

CHILD SEEING

To see as a child sees
too small to walk far
just to sit where we are
and try to fathom what we see
with wonder at our own nativity,
not plumbing depths, searching for stars
nor picking at our adult scars
nor fearing our naivety.

Just sitting still and trying to see
where one begins and other ends,
if anything is itself discreetly,
or if the truth is everything tends
to flow together. Our whole being
one picture with *dazzling* sparkles.
Child seeing.

AN ASIDE/ A LITTLE SONG FOR DANIEL

Excuse me Miss Christine,
please don't be annoyed
but your noisy smelly chickens
just woke up my little boy

Send them to the country
I beg you please do
or I'll cut off their heads
and use them for stew

They poop on my doorstep
and peck my dog's food.
We don't like your chickens
they're noisy and rude

Send them to the country,
if you don't you will see
I will use them for soup
for the baby and me.

ALL SAINTS

The flickering candles on the moonlit graves,
bone fragments still in stockings
on the sand at Choc,
the tiny mice that run round wreaths
down holes to find what homes beneath
the gravestones.

One sails these tidal waves
in a frail boat, and if one's built it wrong
one fails, the failure there
not just the maimed song
but surrender to the sea.

One could die of poetry,
be unmade in a failed making.
Some wall's protecting me.
I try to beat it down
to be willing to drown.

ST JOSEPH AT THE MUSIC SCHOOL

The wind sussurating the shak-shak trees
almost drowning the sounds of the sea
and the children performing for teachers
in the building behind me.
My small son suffers his lesson
silently.
The perfect turquoise of the bay
a green arm of the harbour with a frilled cuff
where the surf breaks on Tapion rock.
The soothing breeze that shakes the trees
blowing gently round my knees,
grapefruit shine yellow in dark leaves –
it is enough.
It has to be enough.

Yesterday
we heard the archbishop say
Saint Joseph is the patron
of a happy death.

THE ACTING DEAN

(For the Miami Caribbean Summer Institute Poetry Workshop, 1993)

The workshop is breaking up
Five weeks of being closer than we knew
jerkily coming to a close.
One by one we disappear
behind the curtain of our daily lives
Everton says we won't see each
other again until we die...

Is that what he said?
Or is that in my head?
I don't recall that he implied
resurrection
but that's the kind of magic that goes on
when eleven damn fool poets
gather daily
allowed to feel for once
that nothing is more important.

It's a kind of nudist camp.
(For Nuala I would have put down nu
dist/camp)
where we can tenderly examine
all the bumps and flaws,
forgetting we are nude

Only at the public readings
are we shocked
into remembering that.

Oh, I wanted to do a stanza for each of you
like one ne(cess)arily
for Nehessiou
and a dark one for Claudia

a very short one
like a gun shot, for Mervyn,
a limerick for Carl just for fun
and for Karen, puns

Durm-I already has a whole poem
and Pat a private one
and all of my poetry
is secretly dedicated to Kendel
but the curtains are closing too fast

and on Monday I will put on business clothes
put up my walls
and walk unsteadily
into the halls
of bureaucracy.

I will put on my acting bureaucrat hat
and say No to everyone
that automatic bureaucratic rattattatic NO
and I will not write
because if I let myself feel
in that wheeled and swivelling plushy chair
my spirit will congeal.

PHANTOMS OF THE OPERA

Energy of stepping straight out
into Broadway's sudden blare
cacophony of people in
a world of theatre where
all the world's a stage in truth.
Audience and players share
the spotlight
daylight / nightlight
in the brittle acid air.

Dark buildings hide lives of
poverty so profound that
the smell of tripe and liver
that meshes you around
is the smell of people cooking
their own innards to survive.
They are eating themselves slowly
They are hiding underground
Then they put on actors' faces
and join the Broadway crowd.

PERFORMER LOOKS AT GRANT WOOD'S AMERICAN GOTHIC

They are visions of rectitude
stiff upper lips, straight backs,
shoulders that can be put to wheels
noses that have been sharpened on grindstones.
Is that their church behind them or their home?
He keeps her soul good.
She watches him carefully
to see what she can think.
He looks out. Straightfaced.
Erect. Admits no doubt.
Is he erect in other places too?
Undoubtedly. Not to be would be a sin.
He has to multiply and increase
and he will if it kills him.
Or her. He holds a trident
pitchfork, dead upright.
Victims of rectitude.
Pillars of spite.

SMALL ISLAND COMMUNION

1. Sausages egg and bread, all ready
together, at the moment when the coffee
pot coughs and gurgles with the rush
of wind, the coming of the Holy Ghost.
Break fast
communion served
with love to trusted friend
companion of the night to the day's end.
Praise the bruised Christ.

2. We are a bad, a sickly people, we
live too close to government to see
how such mastering makes us cling to slavery.

Instead of seeing how we are enslaved
we let ourselves scapegoat some age-old schism –
racism, classism, ghost of colonialism.

Brown-eyed child, trust yourself to be,
to find out what it is that you can do
and do it well. Have mastery
whether or not you're master. Truly be free.

3. The living legacy of the bruised and broken God is this:
suffering as we are, betrayed, always, by a kiss,
pulled in four directions
head tending still towards the heavens
feet to earth, each hand pointing
to one or other thief, ribs disjointing,
begging the Father to take this cup away,
knowing he will not, still
trying to keep wholeness through the grave,
do what we have to do. Suffer. Save.

Make breakfast perfectly
and serve it well.
Whatever good we do
flies in the face of hell.

THE PERFORMER'S PRAYER IN THE CATHEDRAL OF ST. JOHN THE DIVINE

In the flickering light of the vesper candles,
                                                  help me

with the blood beat of the migraine in my temple
                                                  help me

with the feelings that I try to hide from you
                                                  help me

because what I hide from you, I hide from me too,
                                                  help me

because I am lost in this strange century,
                                                  help me

because we are all alone and corrupt,
                                                  help me

because there are too many of us so we look
        and do not see,
                                                  help me

because we are blind and in need,
                                                  help me

because the moon is still beautiful, suspended out there
                                                  help me

because there are beautiful places to be,
                                                  help me

because we still have each other, strangely,
                                                  help me

NEGLECT

Shrivelled by time to a child's dimension
in a shape like a long-past lover, he
raises his arms to her – a pleading meant

to enchant. Fearful, she hesitates. She
looks at her disapproving husband, to
her mother, but can't resist. Lifts, gently

raising to her heart a once loved face, through
years apart familiar, now pallid, ravaged.
Gaining her breast, he elongates. Grows to

monstrous sinewy length that she can't manage.
Lanky limbs flopping out of his control
he clings trustingly. She staggers. A world rage

bellows. Howling dogs loosed, track his bones.
She tries to lay this awful burden down
lovingly, to arrange him on the stones

but the dogs are closing and the ground
uneven. Frantic now, she folds him –
bundle of beloved bones. She flounders

then stuffs the pulsing package deep into
her clothes. Hard against her belly, he quakes,
she dodging dogs round rocky yard, his thin

presence never again to be shaken
from her. She should have held him first time round.
Who knows how much of him time has taken?

THE SEVENTIES

Once we had blown the police station
to happily-gone-away
we got stuck in the crater that was left.
Climbing out, up its earthy, rooty sides
a narrow steep pathway,
trying to help the grumbling little ones
on to the road
we were sideswiped by a runaway cop
under his own steam
travelling horizontal, feet first,
doing sixty.
Head raised to peer at his flying boots
long oo-oo-oo-oo-ooh
of surprise and anticipation
as he whooshed past,
catching me lightly on his shoulder
with big clown feet.

Change isn't always
neat or complete.

I CANNOT FIND THIS ISLAND

I cannot find this island lovely in drought.
I love it best all silvergreen with rain
when clouds creep off La Sorciere
and down the Morne

Right now it is a waste land
creaking in drought.
We live merely by willing it;
our sins have found us out.

I wish I was a priestess
in some vast pyrrhic cult
dancing howling round a churning fire
that never would go out

burning sweet smoke to join a cloud
and make a path through doubt
bawling incantations
screaming for rain

to see this island once again
emerald, shooting rainbows
through the rain, shimmering
in silver cloud rings

or moonlit midnight's deep sapphire
with silver leaping in fish-flashes
from the blackened sea.

FOR A POET WHO CANNOT SPEAK SOBER

I think that, as a child, your toys were words
and like all games, they were much more than toys:
stories you wrote or read became your worlds.
Your living spaces, unlike other boys',
were inside you. The world outside seemed strange.

For babies, strangeness is not frightening.
When everything is new, the mind is free
to range outside itself, play with the lightning,
return to itself with new things seen,
like shaking a kaleidoscope.

No need to understand it.
What has been is gone.
Children do not need hope.

But somehow as you grew, I think what happened
is that the words mixed up with people.
What once was joyful, all that shifting pattern,
became confusion.

While others, ageing, seemed to grow more sure,
for you the earth seemed constantly to rock.
You fought with words on paper for a cure
but outside felt the constant earthquake shock.

You knew that things are not fixed down,
but what had once been, as you grew, sheer joy
to explore, transformed, unreasonably,
into a terror of conversation.

FOR AN ALCOHOLIC FRIEND

The demons of the dancing floor came right inside her head:
I'll be your faery lover; I'll dance into your bed.

Clutching her demon lover, she waltzed into ecstasy
The next day when he followed her she didn't even see.

Do you think that no-one likes you? her demon lover said,
I can dance you through the daylight too, I've power out of bed.

She took him first to parties where he helped her through the door,
they spoke wittily to people and performed on the dance floor

Then she took him out to lunch – he made dreary afternoons
feel full of little bright spots like a frantic child's balloons

But soon she was too tired to climb out of her bed.
I can help you in the morning too, her demon lover said.

So she waltzed her demon lover right from wake up into night.
Her belly swelled with devil child; her eyes were far too bright.

She held her demon lover hard to drown the garish light
that ate away her aching eyes; begged him for quiet night.

She said: Take me away from this! He said that she would see
and her belly burst, poured blackened blood, and finally she was free.

But sometimes in the darkest times, her songs float back to me,
whispering: Save me? Help me, someone. Is there no-one who can see

how the light scares and the dark scares when they glare outside me?
Why must they come inside? How live with that and remain free?

ABOUT MOTHS

She had always wondered why they'd
so repeatedly fly into the staring vertical eye
of the candle's naked flame.
Shuddering, scorched, delicate wings torn
they lurch at it staggering,
time and again.

She had always wondered why
until she woke up one day and realised
she'd always done the same.

A TURTLE LIKE ZEUS

Yelling, presumably:
"Give me Liberty
or give me
Death"
in Turtle,
Lana leapt from the balcony rail.
Green Daniel, who had ignored her for months,
went into a decline.
Wouldn't eat,
wouldn't bask,
just sulked in the green water
growing mossy.
They're all a bit like Zeus, aren't they?
Either ignoring you or being bossy,
but if you disappear, fearing themselves
at something of a loss.
Could any of them say what they want us for?
If you ask them, they get cross…

CHICKEN FEATHERS

They say birds of a feather
flock together
and apples don't fall
far from trees.
Though sometimes a bad apple creeps in
– or a black sheep…
Still, you can set a thief
to catch a thief.

But watching chickens flocking
though they all wear yellow stockings
and are feathered (as are sparrows
and chicken hawks and crows
with whom, goodness knows,
no chicken goes)
some are black with or without sheen
some are brilliant orange and iridescent green
some are plain and soberly white

but the colours they preen
don't seem very much to matter.
They'll flock with any other chicken
who's the right shape
to end on a platter.

THREE FOR D

I. Soul as onion

How does it work?
I watched my grandfather
stroke after stroke
diminishing until
he was hardly there at all.
A wizened shell.
One day the porridge ran down his throat,
one day it flowed down his thin stubbly chin.
That was the only way we could tell.

But what is it that happens?
Does god peel back the layers
one by one until they're all undone?

Is that harsh, shrugging, scratchy sound
the rough stuff of your graduation gown
splitting and tearing?
Will your wedding dress be next?
Might its white chiffon fly
like a ghost butterfly?
Might it make something beautiful
somewhere for someone else?

Will layer by layer be stripped
and all the things you'll miss –
the broderie anglaise
of your babies' christening dress,
the stiffness of their first
communion gowns –
will you sit still and stare
as they are peeled and dried
and flutter off somewhere?

And layer by layer
as that tender shining naked onion dome
is pared back to nothing,
does it revert to what it was in the beginning?
Does your soul seed fly home?

II.

What would I wish for you to fill
these aching empty days? Where time
must sometimes seem so slow and yet
we know it won't be long until…
I find it still unsayable.

You say you miss the classes and I feel
you should come back although you're ill.
No time can be wasted now, after all;
but at least you've moved beyond
the foolish make-work that we feel we have to do.

I hope that you have prayer
and relief from some pill
but most of all I hope, I hope
there's joy in something still –
computer games or plants to grow –
something, some simple joy to kill the time –
the time that creeps along and one day will stand still.

III. *Approaching St. Jude's*

St. Jude's the patron saint of what?
Not, as I think, lost causes?
Please God, not…

The yellow love vine winds
around the shorter bush;
only tall trees stand
mournful above the herd.

I wonder if the taller trees
watching the spindly saplings
struggle, turn brittle brown and die

feel helpless as those driving
down to see the young ones
tangled in love weed, hopelessly
strangled by love vine
when their life was just beginning.
It is hard, St. Jude, too hard,
to see the love vine winning.

MEMORIES

Stepping into sudden twilight
from a cloistered afternoon,
blackened trees etched against a pale blue sky,
transports me back to four years old.
My mother had a dress
of just that blue with black felt
trees embossed
her other blue, the peau de soie,
whose name we thought funny…

But always, early evening,
the past flies back to me
and only love and poems
can keep and fix it there –
my daddy in his dancing shoes
the smell of Mummy's hair

from

FELLOW TRAVELLER (1994)

WASH DAY

Sorting the laundry
into piles off dark and light
thinking about the theory
there should be no spot
of colour with the white
or of the contrary
which holds that black
is soiled far worse
by linty flecks

but laziness wins out.
To follow this philosophy throughout
I'd have to wash each item
separately
and ideally dismember some clothes
and they'd never sew back whole.
This flowery blouse
must be distressed by dresses
that can classify themselves in piles so pure
either can kick her out.

Flowered blouse, I'm trying to decide
where to hide you.

Have you heard any news?
I hear some stupid white hate group's arrested
for wanting to assassinate black leaders
starting with a man called King, whose beating
got a whole race rioting.

Putting his good pale shirt
in with my bras, white towels
I turn black leggings inside out
so lint won't show.

I saw an article in *Time*
how police flagged down a man for speeding
how his pickup truck smelled funny
so they lifted his tarpaulin
to find out what he was hauling
was a decomposing dummy.
        She was nobody's mummy
        and had long since stopped bleeding.

At last he stopped
no doubt relieved, thinking: fair cop.
He showed them where another sixteen lay
concealed.
Calmly agreed.
he could identify the slack
slimy bits of some chick that they
had fished out of the river
five years back
no one had claimed her
it took her killer to name her.

White hot iron hissing
not one of those eighteen
ever
reported missing.

Perhaps some time
some housewife sorting socks
and wondering why
there are always so many odd ones
looking out a window
sees a gap
where an absolutely lone
painted lady used to bloom
and wonders
Yes, and where do teaspoons go?

Flowered blouse
I'm putting all the washing in one load.

Thousands of birds are
flying through an orchard. They
do not touch the fruit.

I fear a certain rancid taste in songs of slavery
although it is not hard to feel the grumbling ships
wallowing sluggish across the ocean with those
holds of misery.

And below decks the reek of blood and bile and vomit
from cracked lips
corrosive sores from rub of salting chains and where
the ropes had burned
and bright metallic rotting smell of those who wouldn't
face the whips.

Yes, brutal and horrific. Perhaps it's just the way to
say we've not learned?
Something is wrong, when the ring of such horrendous
truth clinks like a tarnished gong.
If these images keep clattering cheap and false, perhaps
they're something we've not earned?

Perhaps we need to understand ourselves before we
sing the victim's song.
Held in our inner darkness there are masters as well
as slaves.
We need to make our pilgrimage to see where we've
gone wrong.

Why we are begging for new masters. What will make
us willing to save
our own rich harvest that is wasting? Ripe fruit is
rotting on the ground. Flies
buzz around it while we wail we are owed something
for ancestral graves

which we have never found. But we could take in the
harvest we are leaving for the flies.
It is fly season. While we sentimentalise, the carrion
eaters circle us, the vulture multiplies.

INTERCITY DUB, FOR JEAN

Brixton groans –
from the horror of the hard weight
of history
where the whites flagellate
in their ancestry
and the blacks hold the stone
and they press it to their hearts
and London is a hell
in many many parts.
But your voice rings true
from the edge of hell
cause the music is the love
and you sing it so well.

And I travel through the country
on the intercity train
and the weather may be bad
but the sperm of the rain
wriggles hope, scribbles hope
cross the windows of the train
and the autumn countryside
has a green life still
and the rain-sperm says
it will come again, it will
it will come, it will come,
it will come again
new rich life from the bitter
and dark and driving rain –
and you run like water
over Brixton soil
writing hope on the windows
bringing light through the walls
like the water you connect
with the light above

like the water writing making
the green life swell
cause the music is the love
and you sing it so well.

Now I cannot give to you
what you gave to me
but one small part
of your bravery
makes me stand up to say
that I want to make them see
that you showed me the way
that the way is me
like the way is you
and the way is we
and the love is in the water
in the wells pooled below
and the love is in the light
on the cold cold snow
and the rain lances down
from the light to the well
and it points to heaven
and it points to hell
and the love is real
make the music swell
cause the music is the love
and you sing it so well.

There's a factory blowing smoke-rings
cross the railway line
you know it took me time to learn
that this country wasn't mine
and I want to go back home
to swim in the sunset bay
feel the water and the light
soft-linking night and day

like the music makes a bridge
but there's joy here too
and I might not have seen it
if I hadn't heard you.
And I hope now I'll be writing
this poem all my life
for the black city world
where the word is a knife
that cuts through the love
and divides up the life.
For you saved me from a trap
just before I fell
cause the music is the love
and you sing it so well.

The Brixton-battered sisters
hissed their bitterness and hate
with their black man the oppressor
and death the white race fate
and their don't want to build
no bridge no gate
and I nearly turned away
in pain and rage and fear
till I heard your voice
ringing clarion-clear
and you burst like a flower
from the sad sad soil
and you blew like a breeze
round the shut-tight hall
and you danced like a leaf
and you sang like a bell
you said music reaches heaven
and music changes hell
cause the music is the love
and you sing it so well.

DIRGE FOR ABU BAKR

They won't pay poets, for, they say, they find
we're fiddling while the Caribbean burns.
Fickle, frail, purple flowers have burst out on the hills
after the long drought. But the people's minds
are still dry.

Outside of church, they believe everyone lies,
bribery and theft are what we ought to do
if they will lead to
wealth, the supreme good.
Their thoughts
are tinder.

I cannot tell whether what I come near is
a political meeting or a religious crusade.
All leaders growl and snarl and threaten
trying to wet down sparks of their own kindling.
Because the people must be made to be good,
leaders need to be obeyed. (And paid.)
In the bush, dry wood
is creaking.

Any poor madman with a gun can easily kidnap anyone,
can hold a government to ransom.
People's worst danger is from looting while the police are busy
shooting madmen. Why?
Well, why not, the people say…
the bosses stole it anyway, if we can get it back this way...
we've learned to grab what we can grab today.
In the bush, the brittle wood
is smoking.

The only ones who seem to have beliefs deny their names
believing that their names have denied them.

Mark their graves with an X.
You do not understand the cross.
They did not understand the other thief.
And all of us have lost.
Far away, in the interior, already the rain forests
are burning.

Nothing is holding us together.
What are we supposed to tell the children?
Not what we say, but what they see will mould them.
We murder art and so
we have no true myths that we could have told them.
Big house. Electric things. A car.
A private jet? These are
the things they learn to cheat for
and when they've got them, learn to steal for more.
The scrubby bush, neglected round the town,
is smouldering.

It was said a long time ago
that the problem with lies
is that if you tell them, language dies.
It is so simple all the children know it.
If everyone believes everyone lies
no one will believe anyone anymore.
The children will not listen anymore.
The growling preacher-politicians know,
say: do what I say because my gun is bigger.
But the bush
is burning.

If we cannot believe each others' words
then nothing we can say will ever be heard.
Teachers, licensed to speak so long as they stayed in school
said: communication is survival skill.
If language dies, it follows we all will.

And we are dying now, though you can't hear me
in your business cocktail party in your clean house on the hill
where you have taken in your friends and are lying to them still,
eating each other's Judas food as you move in for the kill.
Still laughing, feeling smart, but the smoke is drifting in.
Can you smell it yet, above the subtlety of gin? It's your garden
that's burning.

And I sit here and dredge my mind
for a word you will never hear,
for a word I will never find outside.
You have degraded words, so we will die.
All of us. Poets, liars, looters, muslims, madmen, you and I.
You have made truth into a clown
that fiddles though the town's past learning.
I might as well lie down. The town
is burning.

MINORITEASE

A Spanish migrant worker
wandered into Argentina
meandered round a few cantinas
and ended in a square
where
a monument stopped his eye.
He asked a fine moustachioed passer-by
(he had, of course, a Spanish accent):
Who might be that distinguished gent?

The Argentinian could not lose
the chance to strike another blow
for freedom: *He's the hero who showed*
the lousy Spaniards who was boss.

The immigrant did not stop to ponder
what course was politic or correct.
Pulling his pistol from his tattered clothes
he shot the offending statue full of holes.

YELLOW GIRL COUPLETS

Any more yellow girls out there
fed up to their underwear

of the double colour bar
that haunts those with too little tar?

Does it make your stomach burn
when you're in town and every turn

some derelict yells out: *White girl!*
Yet contemplate the abuse he'd hurl

if you allowed yourself to enjoy
the obvious retort: Black boy?

Remember how your mother said
white boys will get you into bed

but just for practice, not for keeps,
so mind you look out when he leaps?

I don't know if you found that true
but think of white boys' mothers too.

Remember how they looked at you?
They let you know you wouldn't do.

Apparently it's only right
that we should bear the brunt of spite

that, being fair, we pay the price
for all the crimes of old dead whites.

Only one compensation's given:
this prejudice is not racism.

It's clear we must possess this grace
because, it seems, we have no race.

KINGSTON RAMBLE

1.

Outside, it's downtown Kingston streets
where feral children grapple with each other
in the appalling dust and heat.

And their mother, Jamaica, like a mountainous woman
tries to rest, fanning herself. Her opulent flesh
untethered, spills over in every direction.

Earrings and bangles and chains of gold
lie luxurious against massive near-ebony breasts
but her bare feet are cracked and her wares have rolled

off her tray and are spilling into the dust.
And all the other lovely island girls will come to this,
longing for luxury, vendors of tarnish and rust.

2.

But the National Gallery
is a triumph of metropolitan bureaucracy,
air-conditioned and stately.

I was impressed. But also disturbed
by the first thing you see – Bob Marley as a tree –
eerie and powerful and dumped,

somehow, hardly displayed. It stands in
the foyer like a coat-rack. They say that Jamaicans
stoned each other when they put it up, then

wouldn't stop fighting till they got
the cute one, that gives him a sexy little bum.
It's nice when a people cares about its art.

3.

I began the Edna Manley
exhibition at the wrong end.
I was drawn by the last painting, see,

and so I lost my husband and my friend
and was sucked into the coils of her mind.
I lost myself, in the end.

(I had not meant to lose my husband in Kingston,
for Jamaica was his first real mistress,
his true love, and I was afraid of her,
and felt, no matter how deep my distress
at his irritation with me, on this, my first trip,
I must stay close to him, or she'd have won.)

4.

She was working on Christ raising Lazarus on the night
she died. Can there ever have been a better metaphor
for faith? How she must have blazed up in the morning,
granted the true sight!

I'm glad I was led by your drawing of your death to the wrong door.
Walking the coiling pathway through the streaming plenty
of your life, the best were the first things I saw,

when I was freshest. It was a long time before I noticed how empty
of people the rooms were. When at last two women came through
an opposite door, they sat and talked of shopping.
Perhaps they were dizzy.

Certainly the work they'd seen, your work up to your
forties was enough to
daze them. They'd seen the famous stuff. That powerful
bull-shouldered Negro
head thrown back, and all the early Moseses and Eves
are enough to
amaze anyone. But, when all is done, if I could go again, I'd go
(and I'd go and I'd go, if I could) I would go round the
same wrong way.
The later pieces did not care if others understood. They
weren't for show.

It is so sure. It echoes with and out of some deep unity
and integration.
You were in the world, and the world was in you, and
your visions whirled
through you and hurled themselves into, having come
out of, too, this strange nation.

I'm glad I saw it knowing that on the night you died
you died blazing your vision of the love and light that is
the world inside.

5.

One day, I will write you a better poem. Some day
the animals and people from my dreams that show me
what the world means
will find their shapes as surely as yours did, some way.

Meanwhile, however rambling this poem may seem,
it tells a story of a trip that really happened.
A real life journey walked into a dream.

And as in dreams, the rambling makes a pattern.

You showed me that the dream country was real
because my images appeared in shapes you'd fashioned.

However sad and hopeless this city world may feel
your pathway curls like smoke all through it. Those who follow
know that only love and art have power to heal.

Caring for dreams and dreamers is the one way we can grow.
And in the middle of your life, I found my man again, and
this is in the pattern too, for suddenly I know

you had a man that loved you well. The background
to this work is trust in love. I want to break down
chattering with it. Security and peace and love are all around.

And that is why I want to end this song where I began –
I'd feared the daytime airline trip would snatch me
from my dreams,
instead It helped to make them clear. I need to celebrate the man

who brought me here. Nothing that's real is ever what it seems.
It's not the solid house, it is the harbour that love makes,
gives us strength to dream.

THE FATHER

My neighbour Albert loves his children,
will stand all Sunday, staring down the yard,
hugging his barely toddling baby daughter,
surrounded by his newly walking son
who still has his baby hair, corn-rowed.

And I have heard him, tipsily, with other men
speaking of fatherhood and how it will be hard
to raise their children just the way he ought to.
Acknowledging the mission, he has won
peace and a place within this world. He is owed.

And I'm a spy, when I look down at them, when
I try to chronicle their daily life in pen. It is hard,
surrounded by their rocky yards, feeling out of my
element, water.
I can only watch and love and write, and hope when
I am done,
I can find, as he's finding, right end of right road.

MADMAN

Why are we so afraid of him?
Because he does the things we want to
and are afraid to do?
Because time and again he will give in

to inner impulse, tears, tantrums, cursing,
throwing things, while we
turn quiet, shrinking fear to judgement,
watching him vent the feelings we were nursing?

He has strayed too far into the shadows
without guide or companion.
Too often now, he trails in with the horror
of the ghosts the shadow knows.

He will not keep up our pretence
of normalcy by day,
so we who act it must reject him
as our first defence.

We pass him over, the thirteenth fairy in the tale,
but like her, he is always there,
our dark side. We know him.
We turn him out and wonder why we fail.

We treat him as the thirteenth. We let our shadow win.
Because we want to push him out,
his ghosts will sneak back in, confronting us.
We make him. He holds our guilt and sin.

NEIGHBOURS

Beneath my bedroom window.
naked children are hunting with sticks.
Each tries to kill a butterfly.
This is not a metaphor:
It is a true thing I can see from my window.
And so what?

Outside, Marlene is washing.
The only time she can boss the house
is when her mechanic is out,
so then she makes her child cry.
She never fails to be rough and unkind to him.
Well, it's hot.

When Celestina lived there,
the blows impacting with her flesh echoed
in her lonely patient silence.
She could not conceptualise
her suffering, tried not to inflict it on us.
She did not.

An Indian doctor lived
here once. He visited me while Miss Flor
was ironing. Shocked us
with a woman he came by
in Casualty. You'd swear a beast tried to eat her…
Miss Flor got

hot. She said: If you know that
man and the things that woman do him.
He join Seven Days and so he
marry she. Say he satisfy.
Leave me seven months pregnant with Paul. When he sleep,
she tie knot

with rope around him. When she
pouring, she catch it in a 'tensil
and give it to him for cocoa.
Her own child say. If you tie
man, he must stay, but you must take what you get. True,
is it not?

If I go by the rumshop
for Miss Jean to sell me some onion
or soap, she will serve me first, and
sudden silence loudly cry:
You don't live here. I write syllabics. What else
have I got?

There are a thousand Rosehills
where I live. The naked children say:
I did tell you not to play by
the white lady butterfly.
A thousand people live by me, but my neighbours?
They are not.

IN THE MARIAN HOME

What is it that they're listening to
that they so stubbornly shun
all our helpless offers of radio and television?

What are they staring at
that they have no need of chat
of cardgames, papers, books, even our news?

They'll get cards from long-absent children
and say: *You keep that for me.*
Give them a gift and they will give it away

or politely hide it so that when they die
you'll find it new and useless like everything you buy.
Soap. Talcum powder. Old people's clothes. Chocolate without nuts.

The vain attempts that we insist on using
to reach those who have shut themselves away
from all our manufactured needs of everyday.

They are so matter-of-fact about death.
Point to an empty bed and they'll say:
Oh yes she died. I think it was last Friday.

Will we too, finally, come to our last pee-smelling home,
sit under Mary's arm and spend all day
just breathing his calm breath?

PORTRAIT

Anya digs her stubby fingers into the holy water,
blesses herself and stumbles to a pew,
and on her knees looks so devout you'd never think, would you,
she'd spend the rest of this blest day intent on crossing you.

FOR MIKEL AT THE CIRCUS

We go to the circus with Mikel
but Mikel is going for us.
Mikel is only one (and a half)
so we're anxious to see what he does.

The big top is set by the cemetery at Choc
and we step from the strong tropic light
into the glittery darkness of an otherworld.

Circles of dusty red gold-fringed chairs
Mikel stares solemn as the oompah blares
"Three green peppers and a
hot pot-a-to..."

The ring is barred to hold the bears
who enter through a passageway from who knows where
trailing floppy buttocks, bear buttocks straw clings to
shuffle heavy through sawdust.
Red and gold women crack whips
and bears do lumbering bear tricks
and Mikel's stare is fixed.

We're almost caught in this most magic
place of pure performance.
Spangled girls who'd sold us candyfloss
pink fibreglass, appear in the spangly-dust
tunnel of the spot foot-juggling

or to be tossed in the air
landing on shoulders three men high
or miracle-muscled to fly
across the tent-room ceiling caught
by silver hands emerging from the gloom

The precious pathos of the magic people make.
The sequined sweat,
sweet energy of perfected accomplishment
action exquisitely timed
almost overrides
the tawdry, almost hides
the poverty, the pimples

and Mikel watches all sternly
intent alike on jugglers, clowns
panthers, tigers, grace, fall down,
absorbed in all that passes
Mikel keeps very still.

So this is life, this jungle jangle?
Strewn sawdust, fur, dung, sequin spangle
all passing by his serious eye,
how separate who can say.
To feed his dreams?

He's in no hurry to react
he doesn't worry what we'll think.
May he stay that way.
May he always watch with wonder
never fear his fellow man
may he learn to fly in dreams
and when waking know he can.

Let him love the life inside him
never let him want to hide.

And help us find Mikel's grace
to love the world from our own space.

FELLOW TRAVELLER

You hear the rain crossing the valley?
You know it will strike us quite soon?
You know how this damn roof is leaking?
Well, of course you must know,
for you holed it yourself
when the wind start to blow
on the day that you said
the damn walls hold you in
and you feel like you dead
and you gone on the roof there, to dance.

You said how you were sure
if you climbed right up high
felt the sun right above you,
your hair in the sky,
you would see far far.
That the walls block you up,
that the walls "paw" you in
and you danced and you laughed.

Now, I was afraid you would fall down.
You said No, and, So what if I do?
Is just safety you want?
I have things I must see
and I can't keep on thinking about you.

But you knew I would stay here inside it.
You knew I would wait for you.
Now I wait and have waited and will wait
but, my dancer, the rain's coming in,
and you see how that big storm is brewing?
Where's my shelter?
I drowning again?

You see you, dancer,
big smile on your beautiful mouth?
You see you, seeker?
Fix the roof.
Or is I moving out.

CLICHES FOR AN UNFAITHFUL HUSBAND

So. The game was worth the candle.
Was the candle worth the cake?
Now you have it and you eat it
Does it make your belly ache?

SAHARA SPELL

In the morning
you lie between me and the sunrise
outlined in gold
as I turn to the sun and you
drawing the warmth of the day
from your smooth-waking body.

Late night and
I lie between the full moon and you sleeping
I draw the blue light
through branches of coconut and cedar
and try to weave a magic
protection around us.

It is the dry season
and from our room,
high by the treetops
we see the yard slopes burnt brown and dead.
The Harmattan blows earth
from the Sahara. The air
is thick with it. Cloudy?
They warn the fishermen:
do not go to sea.
Visibility in the Caribbean is limited
by dust from Africa.

But the pregnant March moon
rainbow-haloed holds water
I will draw on its store
to sustain us through April's fires
and soon

when the rains come,
they will tamp the African soil

into our earth
and there will be greening again.
There will be growing again.

AFTER LANGSTON HUGHES

You are breaking my heart with your dream's defer-
ment. I know it's the way of all men and not
your intent, but there are days when the sense of rot
of the dream gets so hot I'd almost prefer
to be able to move from the heart of the fer-
-ment. Because I feel your pain churn so hot
in my own guts. Because we are one. Not
a cliché. You transfer what you feel like a burr,
seeding your pain in me while you are blaming me,
not meaning to, just indulging the burning.
All these days when you can't speak, I'm learning
to love you more and more because I see
I have to learn that fear is lack of trust.
This terror must be kindling for your dream. It must.

STEP/MOTHER

To you
who always left
the butter out
your sandwiches behind
mouthprints on the milkjug

who
purloined all my hoarded-from-cold-climate stockings
to wear as pixie nightcaps tied in topknots

who wore
my Reeboks to allnight beachparties without asking
and put them back soaking wet

who swore
until you were twenty
that wicked witches ate the walnuts
or anything else expensive that I was trying to save for a special
occasion

who constantly lost
bank books, passports, exam certificates
and said the wicked witches took them too

I hope you know who
loves you.

SUITABLE RAIN

Please tell me that this room is empty.
Lie to me – say that I've left none of my life
here where I stubbornly pack for a plane.
All my new-found lifelong friends,
remind me that the music never ends.
That though we do lose something of our life
we move on taking something we have gained.
Though bleakly. Feeling empty,
in this most suitable rain.

SEINE FISHING – A PAINTING

As a small girl, I was awestruck
when the village men hauled in the seine.
The wonder was not at the power of the men
though that thrilled me
nor for the prodigal bounteous fertility of the sea
though I smelt that.

There was a twinge of agony for the fishes' pain
and I felt that, but more –
mostly it was simply the beautiful shock
of the sudden startling living silvering splashing
flipping flashing shore.

DOMESTICITY

Because I love animals, I have declared
genocide on ticks. And now I poison
myself and the dog in the name of love; it's war.
My living room reeks of the charnel house
because I have won one battle with rats
in the ceiling, and on the mat, a mouse
would testify what we know – even a cat
sweet, soft thing – is not immune
to the killing cycle. It leaves trophies
there as gifts so that
we'll feed it well and love it all the more.
There were roaches and ants in the larder
but toxic gases are easily brought to fight that war.

And if the killer spray catches your own breath
try not to breathe until you've shut the door.
Both sides must have casualties. The stench of death
is needed to make room for more.
Try to tell yourself you're doing good. You see,
birth must also smell of blood
and all conception of the drowning sea.

HOPKINS' HAND WAS NEVER WRONG...

I wanted to write poems that shout like a Van Gogh yellow chair,
like the living yeasty warmth inside a plastic bag of bread,
like the times when midnight's turning finds a warm lover in bed,
or exploding sunlight prisms on entwined shining black hair
and the palm tree's sudden coronet that hails me when I wake
set like a gold-green badge to blaze against blue sky.
To celebrate and integrate the ordinary. So why,
what power is it that intervenes and makes the sure hand shake?

It's not that all this passes; even the hard earth quakes.
In centre's sunk Atlantis the visions will endure.
It's more like irritation with all the small mistakes.
I see, but cannot recreate the pictures seen as pure.
I wanted to be able to write like Yeats had come again.
Instead it seems I'm struggling to live as crazy Jane.

TEACHING EXPERIENCE

Most folk, I think, will never see
a poem useful as a recipe.

POETRY WORKSHOP

Our selves, deep down we think
are poured on paper, twisted and reshaped,
typed on to screens, perfected in black ink.

Our talk is not ourselves. We speak with hands
but not hands-on like potters. We use words
but silently inside our/selves. We understand

too little of what at first we say. We
are wary of being understood by
those who speak to us the ordinary way.

It is a little scary. I once knew
a gentle laughing man
whose art was horror. From his hands grew

knived cocks. Cocks filled with stone.
Vicious phalluses of dead bone.
Was he that man?

TRAVEL SICKNESS

I have always been fascinated by
fainting. The way voices recede from you
while darkness creeps round edges of view
and slowly closes down to centre while
you fight desire to fade. If there were not
nausea always with it, it
would intrigue to feel that cold creep bit by bit
from temples through skull – so cold it's almost hot.

Once, the blackness closed till I was blind
and sounds receded totally. I find
the horror of it was that still the mind
stayed active, though bereft of sense of any kind.
This is what we fear of death, but worse,
it's what we fear in life. Isolation. God's curse.

MOMENTS

Always it's moments glimpsed while journeying past.
A darkened hill beneath pale yellow sky.
A shivering sense of peace. It does not last.

Soft smoke drifts slowly, seen through glass
and misty sheets of silvering rain pass by.
Always it's moments glimpsed while journeying past.

A jostling market crowd – colours, shrill, fast –
vision evaporates without a sigh.
A shivering sense of peace. It does not last.

A pale sun hangs above a blackened mast,
a horror that the self itself will die.
Always it's moments glimpsed while journeying past.

An orange sun and pools of silvered purple cast
on glistening asphalt. A sense of one – not-I.
A shivering sense of peace. It does not last.

A sense of home, of peace. Driving too fast
seeking to lose a sense of sinking by.
Always it's moments glimpsed while journeying past.
A shivering sense of peace. It will not last.

THE LECTURER LADY

She says, assuming all of us Miami-ites as well as
Anglicans, that those of us
who were in church on Sunday August 23rd and not at
home nailing shut doors, taking
down the pictures, will remember that the psalm was 46.
Therefore we will not fear, though

earth be moved and mountains topple into depths of sea, the Lord
of hosts is with us, the God
of Jacob is our stronghold. The lesson for this Sunday then
is: If you would find something
to suck comfort from, you need to make your own community.
Huddled in your broom closet

hiding from maddening winds, whiplash of rain, your death stalking
if you would have a fragment
to clutch salvation from, you should have been at church. Some poem
could then visit you, fly into
your heart like a rosary to hold. Concrete walkways do not
succeed in keeping Nature

out. See here and there small leaves have fossilled themselves into
man-made stone. Yet you have to
make your own. Knowing it will be blown down, broken, overgrown
still, you have to make your own.

A BIT LIKE DAVID

The careful measured cadences
of the Anglican hymnal.
Light quiet vibrations, stillness
between pews in organ's swell;

the Book of Common Prayer and Hymns
Ancient and Modern to
clutch comfort from. Outside the whims
and meanness of those who

rouse in us demons of alarm.
Rising from bended knees
intoning plain chant of the psalm,
we damn our enemies

quietly, gently begging God
to rend them limb from limb,
then bend politely to his rod,
suck patience from the hymn.

SHADOWS

The children woke up screaming *Daddy Daddy,*
there's a man outside the bedroom window,
and waking groggy in the moondark glow
I stumbled out behind him, lurching madly.
Inside my mind a graceful bull was prancing
on the hillside above us. I, too slow
to tell what I could see, wavered below
while he unhooked the power cables, dancing,
and while I watched this staggering show,
the cables fell, ripped through the roof and pinned
me to my bed, afraid to move, useless to go.
Is there a man outside? A bull within?
Or is it, facing changings in our lives, we grow
these differing images for our own sense of sin?

FOR FERGUS

When Fergus was dying, I had this fantasy
that when some people die, they ought to leave spaces
like holes in the air where they used to be.

Walking around quite normally, we'd stumble on these places
and choke and gasp in vacuum till the realisation:
Oh! This is where he was. We need true memories, not
just vague traces.

But well before he died, I'd feel a soul-deep irritation
when he would try to drift and they would shake him,
trying to wring
a little more life from him. I wanted him to go with
peaceful celebration.

I touched his body after they'd roped it in a sheet so
porters could sling
it casually on to a barrow. He was not in it, though we
felt him there
in the room. And walking down a common Castries street, later,
I wanted to sing,

feeling his sudden joyous presence everywhere.
From far beyond his death, amazed, he sent a living
blessing, tingling through the air.

BAG LADY

Holy Saturday. World-wide
thousands of candles.
The Pascal phallus thrust
through the meniscus
of thousands of thirsting fonts.
Giving Earth to himself,
full-grown, Easter morning.

Oh Lord, please come. Lighten all our darknesses
and let us find our home.

Be kind to the old bag lady who
seems glued to the cathedral steps
like a gargoyle. She's not a monster
there to keep you out. She's your mother.
Especially she is all your mother's doubts.
She's growing old. Sagging. Dying.
She is mourning.

Oh Lord, please come. Lighten all our darknesses
and let us find our home.

She's not even all that sure what's inside
her bag anymore. Once she dipped in
and found hidden all the old worn
bonnets that she'd ever knitted you. From newborn
to size two, they were fitted together
like those old Russian dolls. They're lost
in there again, like all the rest of you.

Oh Lord, please come. Lighten all our darknesses
and let us find our home.

Once, long before you knew her,
she was quite a pretty girl. Whirling
light and giddy, never tired
though often foolish and not often hired.
But you'd have liked her then. Remember
when you picked her up in a bar, years later,
when she was trying to stave off middle age?

Oh Lord, please come. Lighten all our darknesses
and let us find our home.

You were not very kind to her.
Outside this masculine festival,
that resurrected body rising in an incense smell
light and cleansed after three days in hell,
she is cradling her bag. It's you
baby, blood-slimy from her womb
on the steps of this cold manger.

Oh Lord, please come. Lighten all our darknesses
and let us find our home.

She is rocking in her earth-womb, cannot
enter the chill tomb of the cathedral
to be born. It's only cold comfort she hears
from the lips of men. She still fears
one that speared her open and left her
oozing tears outside the sepulchre when
she could not find where they had laid him.

Oh Lord, please come. Lighten all our darknesses
and let us find our home.

Oh Lord, please come. Let that light
ignite not just the single eye
of the priest's cathedral candle. We need to want

it to unite us all. When you rise from their font
that is not vulval, for its hymen will re-seal,
let us feel you have embraced our dripping slime.
Heal us all. Let the bag lady come this time.

TRANSITIONS

I dreamt of phallic women – not the ring of a good wife!
The mills of God are grinding slow and small.
Now I am in the middle of my life.

Most days I feel I cannot sing at all.
Dreams are forgotten in a time of change
but if not buoyed by dreams, how to escape the Fall?

For late July, even the weather's strange:
Sahara dust and wind as well as rain.
Without our willing it, life has been rearranged.

The mills of God. They churn behind the rain.
The laurels wither on the prizewinner's grave.
It is a Dying Season once again.

Death does have seasons. He rides up in waves.
Some of us are swept out on waves of power.
Do they leave flowers mouldering on the graves

as grisly reminders that, every hour,
the corpse beneath the earth is festering too?
Daily, I pass these rain-grey, rotting wreaths, and shudder.

To make decisions, say what you should do,
seems too much hubris in a changing season.
Better hold still as silence, listening for your cue.

The mills grind small, their power beyond reason.
Changes will come, and deaths, through lives like waves
and to protest it is a sort of treason

to deepest selves. At times like these, only the mad will rave.
To stay sane, huddle in a loving bed, and pray.
All will be mad who try to cheat the grave.

Try listening to your dreams. The phallic women say
we have to know both sides before we find our way.

from

IN TO THE CENTRE

JETSAM

As little children playing on the shores
where whitecap wavelets come and go
we heard the white anxious whispers of our mothers
against the backgrounds of the tides:
What have we done?
Will they be neither one nor the other?

At first we did not listen to a word they'd say.
Even later, when we entered the bouncing surf,
or when we went to school, we found
we had this much common ground:
If you could fight well enough
you were allowed to play.

A little further on, calmly at first,
we learned how to be mirrors.
It seemed to be the same as the way
the sea's surface would reflect the sky and sun
and say: I can talk like you. I can do anything you do
although it's true I don't look quite like you.

And even when we had to make our way
past the reef's breakers to the blue-black deeps
we still believed that if we could fight, we could play.
But then we heard the first dark whisperings,
because you are neither one thing nor the other
we all shall vomit you out of our mouth.

And we were yellowish froth bubbles, wind-blown.
We were thrown up by depth charges
and jettisoned by the tide
tugged by the moon and burst by the sun
seeking for a place world wide.

Now, I, flotsam, having been rolled in the tidal depths,
been tossed by surface breakers and pulled at by ground-swells
wash up finally on the beach where I began.
Gasping below the almonds on the sand
I find myself. Like you. Jetsam.

JEALOUSY

Did you think I did not see you
where you crouched in the porch like a bolom?
It was not mother you looked for
but it was woman who felt you there.
Women.
We are all the same.
That is why we cannot share.

Did you think I did not hear you,
soukouyan,
when you hovered watching
by the high glass pane of the door
burning your moth wings on the edges of the fire inside?
And yet,
and yes, if it pleases you,
you did draw away some of my heat.

When you, gaje,
came right into that room
and beat your wings over that bed
night after night
where he and I and love were one –
you knew why my arms encircled his travelling soul.

Men pretend we are separate, unique,
and try to make themselves into the work that they do.
Daytime people.
Women know
that at night, two by two,
when love is right,
we can reach that darkness
where all things are one
in the light.

I think you had forgotten.
It is easy to do.

We are one and the same.
That is why we cannot share.
Your hate for me becomes my hate for you –
be careful how far you dare.
We have to pass the same maji nwè
the way home.
And I will always know you are there.

BLUEBEARD

My bluebeard lover mutters in his sleep
dreaming of broad-beamed girls and pirate ships
and every night the key escapes his lips.
Yet I am not supposed to guess the deep
dark secret of his central inner place.
Startled, by day he'll say: How did you know?
as if I'd stolen and used the key to go
sneaking behind the "I love you" daytime face.

If sister Anne were here, we'd freely speak
of lovers we sacrificed, our pain,
but men demand we lock our hearts and weep
in secret, then shut the corpses up again.
But Bluebeard, my darling, you cry in your sleep.
Round the locked doors, the smell of guilt creeps.

THE MISTRESS

This temporary room we choose is green
and restful, though I keep
whiskey in the wardrobe
to make sleep certain. Defence
against a spirit scarcely felt, still unseen.

What I feel most is pride, that I have been
a good wife. I have tried
to keep our house going,
against my inclination, in your absence.
With you again, why do I now feel mean?

Perhaps it is the word "wife" that's mean?
It's dutiful. It's dull.
Against my instincts, I
have used an alien domesticity
to steel myself against your loss. I'd been

trying not to feel sad that you have not been
with me. Now I am with you,
I see you are still far.
I do not want to be your wife.
The ghost I've seen
is somehow in the smell of the bed
where the mistress, I wish that I was, has been.

LOVE POEM

These quiet Sundays we have made a ritual
of feeding and loving.
Making love and food, together,
slippery hands sliding
over plump leg of lamb,
ready to eat, sated with love,
I always feel like singing grace.

We have made the best Sundays of my life.
Lately, I had envied churchgoers.
Always the outsider, I realise
that what I wish I had is
their sense of community.

But lately, we have made Sundays an oasis.
A day of rest
of peace and togetherness.
And if through missing church
I miss the pleasures others know in friendship,
my heart lifts, when we sit to eat
in joy that's pure worship.

VOICES FROM DREAMS

Voices that speak to me in dreams insist
that I must make myself a dress of green.
They feed me symbols I may not resist
even if I can't fathom what they mean.

I understand that I must go these journeys
and that I must relate what I have seen,
but how to sculpt the shapes the self sees
to put you in the spaces where I've been?

To fire a burning with a single spark,
it is the hardest thing I've tried to do.
My dreams are fabulous voyages through dark,
and in the swirling mists I find what's true,
but I have not yet learned to build the ark
that can in safety guard the treasure through.

MANDALA DREAM SONG #1

There is a journey we all have to make
that always seems to be the wrong way round.
We want to climb to reach the light but find
that the way to it is a spiral down.

There is a gift that we all have to take
out of the spiral darkness to the day.
Not singing what we wanted it to say,
it must be given, warped so by the way.

There is a love inside the spiral down,
within a central stalagmited room.
I choose the blue stone from the gems around
and care it upwards through the swirling gloom.

There is a green heart inside the brown tree
that cannot be consumed by any fire
though sometimes when we're burning we can't see
the crystal centre of the heart desire.

The gift we seek to carry to the light
must burst out from the centre like a flower
and though we have to search for it through night
we know the day will come, though not what hour.

ABOUT THE AUTHOR

Jane King Hippolyte was born in St Lucia. She was educated in Trinidad and Tobago, Barbados, St Lucia and Scotland, where she received her higher education with degrees in English, Law and a teaching certificate. She was awarded an MA in Literary Studies at Deakin University, Australia.

She has worked as a secondary teacher in Scotland and St Lucia, then as a senior lecturer in English at the Sir Arthur Lewis Community College in St Lucia where she is currently Dean of the Division of Arts, Science and General Studies. She has also been an assistant chief examiner for CAPE Literatures in English, and has served as a judge and chairperson for the Commonwealth Writers Prize.

She was awarded Witter Bynner and James Michener fellowships at Yaddo, New York and the University of Miami respectively. She was awarded the Minvielle & Chastanet Fine Arts Award for Poetry in 1990 and the James Rodway Memorial Prize, awarded by Derek Walcott for *Fellow Traveller* in 1994.

She has a number of acting and directing credits in theatre and was a founding director of the Lighthouse Theatre Company, St Lucia. She has been active in community service.

Her previous publications are *In to the Centre* (1993) and *Fellow Traveller* (1994) and her work has appeared in numerous journals and been widely anthologised.